PREHISTORIC ANIMALS

Troll Associates

PREHISTORIC ANIMALS

by Rae Bains

Illustrated by Alexis Batista

Troll Associates

Library of Congress Cataloging in Publication Data

Bains, Rae.
    Prehistoric animals.

    Summary: Discusses the evolution of animals in pre-
historic times from one-celled creatures which lived in
water, to fish and insects, to the huge reptiles known
as dinosaurs, and eventually to the prehistoric mammals.
        1. Paleontology—Juvenile literature. [1. Prehistoric
animals.   2. Evolution]   I. Batista, Alexis, ill.
II. Title.
QE714.5.B27   1985   560   84-2735
ISBN 0-8167-0296-9 (lib. bdg.)
ISBN 0-8167-0297-7 (pbk.)

Millions of years ago, the ground shook under the heavy steps of giant lizardlike creatures called dinosaurs. There were dinosaurs of all kinds. They had thorny tails or needle-clawed feet or enormous jaws with dagger-sharp teeth. Some dinosaurs were gentle, plant-eating beasts. Others roamed the land in search of smaller animals to eat.

For more than one hundred and fifty million years, the dinosaurs ruled the Earth. Yet, as big and powerful as they were, they all disappeared. An early chapter in the history of life on our planet had come to an end.

The dinosaurs were the largest animals of the past, but they were not the first. The first animals appeared on Earth long before the Age of Dinosaurs. They were simple, one-celled animals, and they lived in the water of the prehistoric seas.

Slowly, as time passed, new kinds of animals appeared in the seas. Some were prehistoric sponges. Others were more complex animals with shells. Among them were prehistoric snails and strange creatures called trilobites.

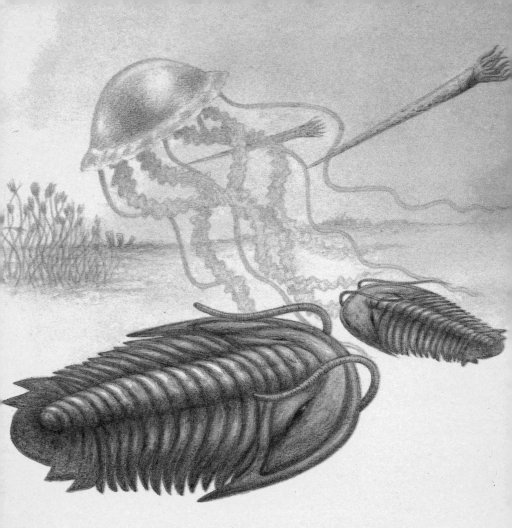

A trilobite had a tough, horny shell. It had more than twenty legs on each side of its body, and it breathed through gills. A trilobite crawled along the muddy sea bottom, hunting for food. If it was threatened, it simply curled into a tight ball, protected by its hard outer plates.

We know about trilobites and other pre-historic animals because of the fossils they left behind. Fossils are any remains of prehistoric plants or animal life. If scientists find seashell fossils in a rock, they know two things. First, a shellfish once lived in the place where the rock now stands. Second, the place where the rock now stands was once covered with water—because shellfish live in water.

Scientists find fossils in rocks, in coal, in tar, and in ice. They also find fossils in amber—a hard, glasslike substance that was once a sticky fluid given off by evergreen trees.

Prehistoric animals that have been fossilized in amber or frozen in ice look exactly as they did when they were alive millions of years ago. A fossil insect now preserved in amber may have landed in the sticky liquid from an evergreen tree and become trapped and covered millions of years ago. The air hardened the liquid, turning it into amber. Inside was the fossilized body of the unfortunate insect— permanently preserved.

In much the same way, larger prehistoric animals have been preserved in ice. For example, a huge wooly mammoth was found frozen solid in the ice of Siberia.

When this ancestor of today's elephants was discovered at the beginning of the twentieth century, it looked exactly as it had looked twenty thousand years ago. Its mouth was still filled with the grass it had been eating when it was suddenly frozen solid!

By studying fossils, scientists can learn many things. For example, by studying the fossil record, they know that trilobites were the most common animals for about one-hundred million years!

Then, gradually, trilobites were replaced by a new kind of water dweller. These newcomers were the first animals with bony skeletons, and they were the ancestors of many of our present-day fish.

As the animal life in the seas changed, so did the plant life on the land. New forms of plants appeared, many of which had green leaves, flowers, and seeds. Along with these new plants came another kind, or class, of prehistoric animal life. These prehistoric animals were the insects.

Some of them were like the insects we know today, except for their size. Some of them were huge. Prehistoric dragonflies had a wingspan of more than two feet. Scorpions were nearly two feet long. And prehistoric cockroaches were as big as modern-day mice!

Then another new class of animals appeared. These creatures looked like fish, but
they didn't act like fish. Each one breathed air
and spent at least part of its life on land.
Scientists call them *amphibians*. This name
comes from a Greek word that means
"double life."

The amphibians led a double life. They hatched from eggs that were laid in the water. The newly hatched amphibians, called larvae, stayed in the water until they had changed into adults. By that time, they had developed lungs, so they moved onto the land and breathed air.

One of the first amphibians was called Diplocaulus. This small creature had a head that was shaped like a triangle! One of the largest amphibians was called Eryops. Eryops was three or four times as large as Diplocaulus and looked something like a fat crocodile.

Long after the amphibians first appeared, another new class of animals developed. These new creatures were the reptiles. They were even better adapted to life on land than the amphibians were.

Reptiles laid their hard, dry-shelled eggs on land. These shells protected the eggs until they were ready to hatch and kept them from drying up inside.

The first reptiles in prehistoric times were probably small and may have eaten insects. But as time passed, larger reptiles appeared. Some were similar to today's reptiles, except that they were much larger. There were prehistoric crocodiles that were more than four times as large as today's crocodiles. There was a giant turtle called Archelon, who lived in the sea.

Other reptiles did not look much like today's reptiles at all. The leathery-winged pterosaurs could fly through the air like birds. The giant ichthyosaurs could swim through the ocean like fish. Other prehistoric reptiles resembled dragons or sea serpents.

Of course, the largest prehistoric reptiles were the gigantic dinosaurs. Some, like plant-eating Diplodocus and Brontosaurus, walked on four legs. Others, like meat-eating Allosaurus and Tyrannosaurus Rex, walked on two legs.

Some, like the duck-billed dinosaurs, protected themselves from their enemies by running for the safety of the water. Others, like Triceratops, used sharp horns to defend themselves from their enemies.

For more than a hundred and fifty million years, the dinosaurs ruled the Earth. But the world continued to change. New kinds of trees and plants developed. So did new kinds of animals, called mammals.

Mammals were warm-blooded animals, with hair to keep them warm, and babies that were born alive instead of hatching from eggs. These were all advantages that helped the mammals survive and become very successful. The first mammals were very small, but larger species developed as the ages passed.

Some prehistoric mammals looked something like modern mice or rats. They were probably timid animals, scurrying about and hiding from the larger creatures that ruled the world. Other early mammals may have looked like small bears or like relatives of today's monkeys.

But some of the mammals looked like no other single animal—past or present. For example, Moropus was a plant-eating mammal that looked something like a hairy, short-necked giraffe, with a horselike head, and with claws on its feet! And Alticamelus was a camel-like animal with a neck as long as a modern giraffe's.

Some prehistoric mammals returned to the sea and became the ancestors of today's whales, dolphins, and seals. Others—the distant ancestors of today's bats—learned how to fly.

But most of the mammals preferred the

land, and remained on the ground. Some of them were like miniature versions of their modern relatives. Eohippus, or "dawn horse," is one example. It looked something like a modern horse, but was only the size of a cat!

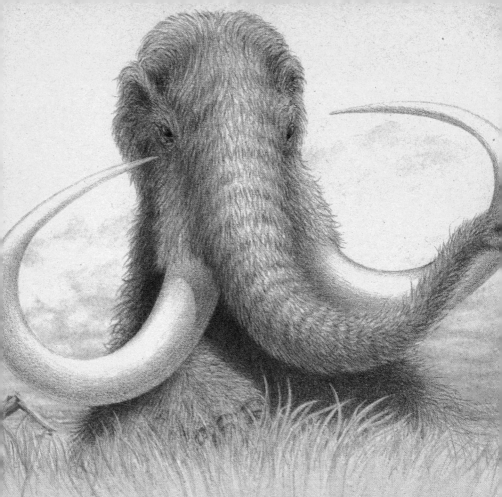

The wooly mammoth, which was a relative of today's elephants, lived during the Ice Age. It had long hair to keep it warm, and it had huge, curved tusks. Early people hunted these enormous creatures and drew pictures of them on the walls of caves. Other prehistoric mammals that existed at the same time as early people included the

wooly rhinoceros and a terrible saber-toothed cat called Smilodon.

Ever since the first animals appeared in the prehistoric seas, six-hundred million years ago, new kinds of animals have continually developed. Some have not survived. Others have been able to adapt to the ever-changing world and have thrived.

Some ruled the world, only to be dethroned by other kinds of animals—animals better suited for survival. The dinosaurs ruled the Earth for more than one hundred and fifty million years. The mammals have reigned for about sixty-five million years.

Today, the world is ruled by one single kind of mammal—human beings. But humans have existed for less than three million years. Will we continue to rule for as long as the mighty dinosaurs did?

Only time will tell.